THE SWAYZE YEAR

YOU'RE NOT OLD, YOU'RE JUST GETTING STARTED!

COLLEEN AF VENABLE
& MEGHAN DALY

Andrews McMeel
PUBLISHING®

Andrews McMeel Publishing
a division of Andrews McMeel Universal
1130 Walnut Street, Kansas City, Missouri 64106

www.andrewsmcmeel.com

23 24 25 26 27 CHJ 10 9 8 7 6 5 4 3 2 1

ISBN: 978-1-5248-7511-4

Library of Congress Control Number: 2023931257

Editors: Allison Adler and Melissa Zahorsky
Designer: Tiffany Meairs
Production Editor: Brianna Westervelt
Production Manager: Chadd Keim

For Meghan, who would never let anybody put me in a corner.
And for you, my dear yet-to-find-your-thing readers.
—C.V.

For Colleen, who convinced me that our Swayze Year joke would make a great book, and for my friends who endlessly support me in whatever wildly disparate endeavors I pursue.
—M.D.

INTRODUCTION

You know the feeling. You move and *something* creaks. You wake up with what feels like a hangover when you haven't been drinking. You start saying "9 p.m.? Who meets at 9 p.m.?" Figure skaters are younger than you are, then actors, then musicians, then spokespeople for AARP. A future that seemed infinite suddenly feels very finite. Maybe you start to narrow your dreams. Maybe you start to make excuses. Maybe you use *THE PHRASE*.

I'm too old to take up a new career.

I'm too old to try something different.

I'm too old to find the perfect blend of eleven herbs and spices to start a fried chicken chain.

You need a friend who isn't going to allow you to feel any less worthy no matter how many rings your tree's got.

This book is that friend.

* * *

The Swayze Year came about when Colleen was about to turn thirty-five and was being a whiny baby about it. "Ugh, I'm unmarried! In a job I don't like! And out of shape! But I'm too old to make any real changes!" Meghan—her best friend since college—pointed out that Patrick Swayze was thirty-five when he got his big break, kicking *really* high in *really* tight pants and standing up to anyone trying to put Baby in a corner in the classic '80s film *Dirty Dancing*.

We started to call age thirty-five "The Swayze Year" and began to map out other inspirational figures for each subsequent age—figures who got their big breaks or accomplished incredible feats not when they were twenty or thirty but at age forty, sixty, even one hundred.

This book profiles one person for every year from age thirty-five to age one hundred—people who climbed mountains, metaphorical and literal; wrote their own storylines; and found their "happy little trees," proving that no matter how old you are, you're not done yet.

Like Alan Rickman, who got his first movie-acting role at forty-two in a little-known flick called *Die Hard*. Or Tina Turner, who exploded the Billboard charts in a very tiny skirt at forty-five. Or how about J. R. R. Tolkien, who wrote *The Lord of the Rings* at sixty-two? Or Jackie "Moms" Mabley, who was the first Black female stand-up comedian to land a gold record at sixty-seven? And you should definitely be inspired by Teiichi Igarashi, who climbed Mount Fuji at ninety-nine.

If you take anything away from these stories, we hope it's that birthdays aren't something to dread but instead are opportunities to try new things and keep following your dreams. Colleen wrote this book in her "Ball'er Year." (At age forty, Lucille Ball became a household name in *I Love Lucy* and was damn stunning even when shoving conveyor-belt chocolates into her mouth.) And Meghan wrote this book in her "Steal Your Moments Year." (At age thirty-nine, Toni Morrison published her first novel, *The Bluest Eye*, and punched the world in the gut with her brilliant and eye-opening writing.)

These lighthearted, humorous bios and inspiring stories are meant to help you get out of your own head, laugh, and hopefully restore a sense of optimism and possibility. Don't fear the calendar. It's never too late to get started.

35
THE SWAYZE YEAR

What? You think you're OLD?

Some days you may feel like you're a pachanga in a world of tangos—like you missed your chance to make a mark on the world. But, like Baby's dad judging Johnny in *Dirty Dancing*, you couldn't be more wrong.

Stop thinking you missed your chance. Put on your dance pants, kick those legs up high, and don't forget to lift up your friends.

You're not old. You're just getting started, and baby, nobody can put you in a corner.

* * *

Patrick Swayze pursued multiple artistic endeavors in his youth, including dance and performance. He landed his first movie role at the age of twenty-seven in *Skatetown USA*, a star-studded flop, which turned him off dancing as a career . . . especially on roller skates. But fate wanted those hips to gyrate and at age thirty-five he returned to dance and landed the gig of a lifetime in *Dirty Dancing*. Swayze's Johnny defied physics in very tight pants, and slumber parties all over the world wore out their VHS tapes trying to pause on the half-second view of his glorious side-butt.

36

36

THE GO TO ELEVEN YEAR

Most years only go to ten. This one? This one goes to eleven.

While you may have a higher chance of spontaneous combustion this year—especially if you are a drummer—year thirty-six is filled with possibilities. Like, when's the last time you rocked out to your favorite song? Or visited majestic Stonehenge? Or put a cucumber in your pants? Live a little! Or die a little! (You know, that whole spontaneous combustion thing.)

Take the stage. You own it.

* * *

Christopher Guest was born into an aristocratic life of privilege. His parents focused on worthy creative pursuits like his clarinet and mandolin studies rather than anything having to do with comedy. He split his time between England and America, mastering both accents, which came in handy when at age twenty-three he decided to become an actor. After years performing Off-Broadway, Guest finally turned his amp up to eleven by co-writing and starring in *Spinal Tap*, leading to his long career in mockumentaries and the beautiful cinematic line, "You can't really dust for vomit."

37

37

THE (IT'S TOTALLY A) FLOWER YEAR

Pick up that pencil or pen or paintbrush or . . . hey, wait a minute?! Why do all art supplies look like penises?! Has anyone else noticed this? I'm gonna take this complaint all the way to Washington! All right, I'm here in Washington and . . . what is that giant thing in the middle of the National Mall?! We hope someone has done *something* to even this out.

This is your year to say, "Damn the Man!" Get in touch with your creative side, your feminine side, and your cow skull side. Make some art. The world needs more of it.

* * *

Georgia O'Keeffe grew up one of seven kids on a farm in rural Wisconsin. At an early age her teachers noticed her talent for drawing and painting. She was accepted to the Art Institute of Chicago but contracted typhoid fever and was out of school for a year. She eventually recovered and went on to teach art in public schools, leading her to the American Southwest, which inspired her unique fusion of realism and abstraction and cemented her role in the American modernism movement. At age thirty-seven, Georgia O'Keeffe exhibited the first of her famous "flower" paintings and became a household name beyond the art world.

38

38

THE ONE GIANT LEAP YEAR

Do you feel like you need a vacation? Why don't you take a long trip this year? I hear the Sea of Tranquility is lovely, and your burdens will feel 85.5% lighter. Explore something new and walk with an extra spring in your step. Join forces with a friend or two and make your mark on the universe.

This year, take small steps, but make giant leaps.

* * *

Neil Armstrong moved so much when he was a kid that his best friend was an airplane. He was six years old when some adult let him fly his first plane and he decided to dedicate his life to flight. Little did he realize he was preparing himself to soar beyond our skies. Aeronautical engineer, fighter pilot, high-speed test pilot—sure, those are all great jobs, but what are they compared to being an astronaut? Though he was a man who loved being in the air, it was a walk that cemented his place in history when, at age thirty-eight, he became the first human to walk on the moon.

39

39

THE STEAL YOUR MOMENTS YEAR

There are words inside of you that need to get out. So what if you have a demanding job or two? So what if you have small children or a family or a spouse who demands your time? Because "your time" exists. Find those minutes hiding between your tasks. Carve out space for yourself and your voice. Notice the stories that have yet to be told and help amplify them.

This is your year to speak up, to look at the past with new eyes. You are beloved. And your stories have power.

* * *

Toni Morrison's father worked three jobs to support the family during the Great Depression and life was difficult. But things turned around for Toni when she learned to read. She devoured books and eventually earned a scholarship to Howard University. *The Bluest Eye* began as a short story she wrote in a writer's group at Howard nearly twelve years before it was published. After graduating, Morrison found success working behind the scenes as an editor at Random House, but she didn't give up on her dream. She would wake up at 4 a.m. to write before the demands of work and being a single mother stole her day. But finally, at age thirty-nine, Morrison published her debut novel, *The Bluest Eye,* and went on to become the first Black woman to win the Nobel Prize.

40
THE BALL'ER YEAR

The conveyor belt of life is coming at you hard and fast. What are you going to do? Just walk away? Hell no! Shove those sweet nuggets in your face! Down your shirt! Down your best friend's shirt! Because you really do have the best friends.

Doesn't matter your gender, this is your year to be a boss bitch. Run the show, dance to the beat of your own conga drummer, and stomp the grapes of your enemies.

* * *

Lucille Ball's father died when she was around three years old, and her mother remarried and sent Lucille away to live with her strict, humorless step-grandparents. She dropped out of high school, hoping to make it in vaudeville. She worked as a showgirl for many years, trying to catch a break, but ended up with the nickname "The Queen of B-Movies." It wasn't until she was cast as a "zany housewife" in a CBS radio program that her star began to rise. They offered her a chance at a TV show and Ball developed *I Love Lucy*, insisting on working with Desi Arnaz, her real-life Cuban-American husband. She was forty when *I Love Lucy* became a huge success and was the first TV show to portray an interracial marriage. Ball went on to become the first woman to run a major television studio.

41
THE HAPPY LITTLE YEAR

Oh, hello. We're so glad you could join us. Thanks so much for coming. Are you ready to make some art? We know you are. All you'll need is one happy little tube of titanium white, three fan brushes, sixty-three palette knives, and at least five cans of Aqua Net. Gotta look good for all those happy little friends you'll be making.

Stare at fluffy cotton clouds. Revel in perfect pine trees. Thwack those brushes. Find the highlights on those snowcapped mountains. There are no mistakes, just happy little accidents.

* * *

Bob Ross was raised in Florida—which officially makes him the best thing to ever come out of Florida—and he dropped out of high school after one year to help his father in his carpentry business. Sadly, that job ended in Ross losing half of his left index finger, but that accident didn't seem to dampen his infectiously cheery spirit. When he was eighteen, he joined the Air Force and was stationed in Alaska, where he saw beautiful snowy mountains that stayed in his heart and influenced his art for the rest of his life. Ross took his first painting class while in the Air Force and fell in love. He decided to pursue painting full time, but it wasn't easy. He struggled for years and was so broke he decided to perm his hair to avoid paying for frequent haircuts (a choice he would later regret). At age forty-one, Bob Ross and his giant signature perm finally landed a happy little role as the host of *The Joy of Painting* and taught the world to paint.

42

42

THE SHOOT THE GLASS YEAR

There's always at least one person who's going to get in your way. You know the type—wise-cracking, duct-crawling party-crasher who always has to have the last word. But you have plans, big plans. And no one—other than that one guy—is going to stop you.

This is a good year to rethink your financial strategy, learn a new language (or at least the accent for it), and perhaps even fall for someone.

And fall. And fall.

* * *

Alan Rickman's spell-binding voice and elegant vocal cadence made him a star, but both these things came from a place of struggle—he had a speech impediment and jaw problem as a child. Before he was everyone's favorite grumpy Hogwarts professor, Rickman worked as a graphic designer, owning his own firm. He started to take acting classes at the Royal Academy in his late twenties, and his teachers there told him his voice was too strange for him to be successful. He didn't give up, and his teachers were proven wrong when Rickman and his hypnotic voice received a Tony nomination for his performance as the villain in *Les Liaisons Dangereuses*. However, it wasn't until age forty-two that he finally starred on screen in his first movie role as the iconic Hans Gruber in the action classic *Die Hard*.

43

43
THE GLOW YEAR

"The glow year? Wait . . . you're pregnant?!"
"Nope. Radiation." ***WINK***

* * *

Marie Curie was raised poor in Poland, and her mother died when Marie was only ten. Even though she was brilliant from a young age, sadly, higher learning wasn't an option as women were not allowed to go to university in Poland at the time. So she ravenously read textbooks to learn what she could herself and attended illegal underground "university" classes. Unable to even afford heat, Curie did odd jobs and supported both her sister and herself, eventually landing a job in Paris, where she earned a spot studying at the Sorbonne. At age thirty-one, Curie discovered radium along with her husband, and they shared the Nobel Prize for physics when she was thirty-six, making Marie the first woman to receive the honor. Eight years later, at the age of forty-three, she won again, this time a solo award for chemistry. She was the first person to ever win twice.

44

44

THE UNBOUGHT UNBOSSED YEAR

It feels bad when people tell you that you aren't capable of something, but it's even worse when you tell that to yourself. Don't let the naysayers hold you back, including the itty-bitty naysayer in your head. Step up and try something new this year. Break out of the box society has built for you.

It's not only time for a radical change—it's time to BE the radical change. Plow your way to the top, clearing a path for a whole slew of others to follow. You are strong, you are a smart, you are unbought and unbossed.

* * *

Shirley Chisholm was born to immigrant parents in Brooklyn in the 1920s. Her parents, a factory worker from Guyana and a seamstress from Barbados, sent her to Barbados at a young age to be raised by her grandmother. But New York City was her true home, and when she was old enough, she returned, earning a spot at Brooklyn College and graduating at the top of her class. One of her professors was impressed and encouraged Chisholm to get into politics (what a smart professor!), but she declined, assuming that as a woman, especially a Black woman, she'd never be given space to succeed. Instead, she spent the next eighteen years working in early childhood education, earning a master's degree in education from Columbia while working as a preschool teacher. She went on to consult for the NYC Division of Day Care, which ignited her political drive. Shortly thereafter, she ran for and was elected to the New York State Assembly by appealing directly to women voters, and four years after that, using her famous campaign slogan, "Unbought and Unbossed," she became the first Black woman elected to Congress. Chisholm made it her mission to create opportunities for future female leaders by exclusively hiring women to work in her office. She was a congresswoman for seven terms and went on to become the first woman to run for president in 1972. This Shirley IS serious (see entry 54). Seriously awesome.

45

THE SOLO YEAR

Look around you: Are you being held up? Is something—or someone—holding you down? Do you control your own path? Do you know your worth? Do you own at least one outfit covered in lots of fringe-y bits that wiggle like an excited Muppet when you let loose and dance?

This is your year to dump that excess baggage weighing you down. Sometimes it's better to go it alone, and when you do, you may find the whole world starts singing your song.

You're simply the best.

* * *

Tina Turner was the youngest child born to sharecroppers in a small town in Tennessee. Her early days were filled with uncertainty, instability, and, sadly, abuse. But she found solace in music. Turner sang in the church choir, and when she was sixteen she moved to St. Louis, spending her nights listening to bands, including her favorite, The Kings of Rhythm, led by her future ex-husband, Ike Turner. One night someone handed her a microphone, and the rest was history. No one could believe that such a powerful voice was coming out of Tina's tiny frame. They immediately asked her to join the band, married her (just Ike, not the whole band), and together they ruled the '60s and early '70s with hit after hit. But Ike was a jerk. That's right, we said it. A JERK. He was abusive and addicted to drugs, and Tina finally broke free in 1976. For nearly a decade, she continued to perform solo but was considered a nostalgia act, performing mostly at hotels and small clubs. All that changed when she released her comeback album, *Private Dancer*, in 1984, and solidified her place in music history. The album would sell eleven million copies, win three Grammy Awards, and stay in the top 100 for over two years, proving that Tina Turner is, in fact, simply the best.

46

46

THE KNOW RESPECT YEAR

Are you sitting down? Have you tried . . . stand-up? Hey-o! Is this thing on? Tip your waitstaff!

Okay, so we aren't all natural comedians. But most of us deserve a second chance and some respect. Perhaps this is the year you go back to school or learn to golf or run a soccer team where you force children to wear wigs and cheat.

There are a whole lot of hecklers in this world. Ignore them or, better yet, catch those tomatoes, take a bite, and throw 'em back, you glorious weirdo.

* * *

Rodney Dangerfield was born Jacob Rodney Cohen in Long Island, NY. His father, a vaudeville performer, was rarely home and eventually abandoned the family. As a child, Dangerfield delivered groceries, sold ice cream, and shilled newspapers—anything to help make ends meet. At nineteen, he changed his name to Jack Roy and tried his hand at writing comedy, but it didn't pay enough, and he quit show biz to sell aluminum siding. Years later, the jokes were still tickling his brain, so he thought, "Hey, I could do both!" He worked as a salesman by day and performed at night, eventually booking gigs on the Catskills circuit. But he still struggled to find his niche in the industry, so he honed a new stage persona and "can't catch a break" Rodney Dangerfield was born. He mastered the one-liner and steadily gained fans. And that's when Rodney actually *did* catch a break, when *The Ed Sullivan Show* needed a last-minute replacement for another act. Dangerfield was a hit and soon became a household name. He performed on *The Tonight Show* more than seventy times and continued to act and perform for the rest of his life, starring in movies like cult favorites *Caddyshack*, *Back to School*, and *Ladybugs*.

47

47

THE BEAM ME UP YEAR

To infinity and beyond! What? Wrong franchise? Sorry! We meant, In space no one can hear you scream. Still not the right one, and more scary than inspirational? Hmmm. How about: blah blah blah Kessel run in something, something parsnips. No?

We swear we watched *Star Trek: The Next Generation*! It's just that with Patrick Stewart front and center it was hard to notice anything else. Maybe there was a robot guy, a cat, a trombone, and Whoopi was there and she had a rad milliner. We're not entirely sure because mostly we were just waiting for O Captain, My Captain to grace the screen with his sexy baldness.

This year, take charge and explore. Travel somewhere you haven't been. Embrace something once considered a sign of aging and realize it's just you getting sexier with every day. Make it so. And don't be assimilated by Borgs.

* * *

Sir Patrick Stewart grew up in a poor household in Mirfield, England. His father suffered from PTSD from WWII and took out his anger on his son. Stewart found escape in acting. By fifteen, he left school to pursue his passion, making his way to London. The stage loved him, and he earned a place in the Royal Shakespeare Company and then made his way to Broadway. Stewart started to branch out, and his talent won him many roles on British and American TV series and movies, but he never achieved widespread recognition. That was until Jean-Luc Picard. Stewart was forty-seven when he landed the role that would make him an international household name, but he wasn't convinced the role was going to work out. When *The Next Generation* began filming, Stewart lived out of his suitcase because he was certain the show wouldn't be a success. Thankfully, *The Next Generation* aired for seven seasons plus four subsequent movies, all starring Stewart as the super sexy Captain Picard. Presumably, he was finally able to unpack.

48

48
THE INSTANT YEAR

You're tough, you're accessible, and according to weirdo survivalists on the internet, you have a shelf life of way more years than it says on the package.

And when you find yourself in hot water, you just get more delicious.

* * *

Momofuko Ando was raised by his grandparents, who owned a small textile store, and he opened his own successful textile company at age twenty-two. But when he was thirty-eight, things weren't looking as good. Ando was convicted of tax evasion—which was actually due to him providing scholarships to students—and he served two years in jail, causing his textile company to go bankrupt. His big heart got him in trouble that time, but it was his compassion that would lead to his greatest success. In 1958, Japan was still suffering from post-WWII food shortages. Ando decided to invent shelf-stable noodles, saying, "Peace will come to the world when there is enough food." At the age of forty-eight, after much trial and error, he created Chicken Ramen, the first instant ramen noodles, an inexpensive and long-lasting product the world—and especially college students—adored. A decade later he also invented Cup Noodles, making Ando the king of instant pasta.

49

49

THE SPOOKY SPECTACULAR YEAR

There's nothing you should fear in life. Except maybe aliens. And ghosts. And werewolves. And vampires. Plant clones that look like your father. Haunted masks that give you new murder-y personalities. Ventriloquist dummies that encountered one too many cold hands and now want to be the ones in control.

But all those things are just as imaginary as that little voice telling you it's too late to switch careers or try something new. Explore your options, and think about what would make you happy. If you're a novelist, try writing in a different genre and selling more than four hundred million books. Don't fear anything.

Except dolls. We mean it. Don't mess with dolls.

* * *

R. L. Stine, born Robert Lawrence Stine, was a naturally shy kid, unsure of his place in the world. When he was nine he found an old typewriter in the attic (which sounds exactly like how one of his later books would begin. Eep!). But instead of using the haunted typewriter to write scary stories, he immediately began to write jokes with it—yes, jokes. In college he became the editor of the humor magazine and after graduation, made his way to New York City and landed a job at the children's publisher Scholastic. Using the name Jovial Bob Stine, he wrote joke book novelizations of comedy movies. But his editors asked him to try his hand at writing something scary. In his early forties Stine created a haunting book for teens, called *Blind Date*. It was a hit, and he found his genre. He went on to write other horror books, but it was his *Goosebumps* series, first published when he was forty-nine, that took the world by the haunted puppet strings. Selling more than four hundred million copies and adapted into both a wildly popular TV show and movie, *Goosebumps* scared the pants off kids across the globe and taught us all you're never too old to try something new.

50

50
THE EVOLUTION YEAR

It's time for a change, and change is good. We didn't get this far by dragging our arms. Stand up straight and work that fire. Open your eyes to new things, and maybe even grow a few more. Like creepy big cat eyes that can see in the dark. Or spider eyes just piled on your face in ridiculous numbers. Or just get rid of your eyes entirely, go live in the bottom of the ocean, and terrify small children forced to look at you on school trips to underfunded aquariums.

Point is, you should always be open to growing as a person. Keep evolving.

* * *

Charles Darwin grew up surrounded by science. His father was a doctor, and his grandfather was a well-known poet, philosopher, botanist, and naturalist. He spent his childhood in the English countryside developing a fascination with the natural world. Darwin's father hoped his son would follow in his footsteps and become a medical doctor, but Charles turned out to *not* be a fan of blood, something he unfortunately found out during an ill-fated attempt to study medicine at the University of Edinburgh in 1825. So he turned his attention back to his first love, the living world, and focused on natural history. At age twenty-two, he decided he needed to experience more of Earth's flora and fauna and set sail on the HMS *Beagle* for a five-year expedition. Darwin circumnavigated the world collecting plants, animal samples, fossils, and other fancy tchotchkes. This voyage became the basis for Darwin's scientific theories about evolution, and twenty-three years later he wrote his seminal work on the subject, *On the Origin of Species by Means of Natural Selection*, which transformed our understanding of the world and our place in it. Note: He only had two human eyes. Underachiever.

51
L'ANNÉE DU BEURRE

It's a proven fact that there's one thing that makes everything better. World peace? Uh, yeah, world peace would be cool too, but we were thinking BUTTER.

Get to know your kitchen. Experiment with flavor profiles and new techniques. Get creative! Make those chickens dance! And if the thing you're working on flops out of the pan, as Julia Child sagely said, "You just scoop it back into the pan. Remember, you are alone in the kitchen and nobody can see you."

* * *

Julia Child grew up (and up and up) in a wealthy family in California. Eventually growing to 6'3" she became known for her athletic prowess and impish sense of humor. She loved a good joke and good food, but since she grew up with a cook in her rich parents' home, she never learned how to prepare food for herself. It's hard to believe that she didn't even pick up a whisk until she was thirty-two. When she and her husband moved to France—the most butter-loving of all countries—she decided it was time to become better acquainted with the kitchen. Child began taking classes at Le Cordon Bleu and graduated with a wealth of knowledge. She teamed up with her friends Simone Beck and Louisette Bertholle to make French food accessible to the everyday cook, and together they wrote *Mastering the Art of French Cooking*. When the book was published, she appeared on a TV cooking segment to promote it. The television executives were so taken with Child's combination of whimsy and frankness while preparing an omelet, they invited her to tape her own cooking show. *The French Chef* was born, which brought Julia Child into America's heart, and Butter Cuisine . . . that is, French Cuisine . . . into America's homes.

52

52
THE SEXY YEAR

What is life if we don't let ourselves feel? Connect to the physical world this year. Be aware of your body. Focus on each of your senses. The smell of flowers as they drift through the wind. The feel of fresh snow between your fingers. The taste of warm apple pie. The sound of laughter. The view of a sunset.

Welcome the comforting connectivity of touch: all your nerve endings, intertwined, like millions of points in the universe sending messages that unite us all.

Also, try butt stuff.

* * *

Dr. Ruth Westheimer was born Karola Ruth Siegel to a prosperous Jewish family in Germany in the 1920s. As a child, she would sneak into the library to read her father's books. When the Nazis gained power, Ruth was sent to a Swiss orphanage for protection. She never saw her family again. At school, she frequently got in trouble for sharing her knowledge on taboo subjects like menstruation. After WWII ended, she traveled, learned to be a sniper (yes, a sniper), then went on to study psychology in Paris. She got married and divorced, set sail for America, had a child, and got married and divorced again. After a stint as a housemaid—taking English classes and earning her master's degree at night—she landed a job at Planned Parenthood. Ruth worked her way up while earning her doctorate in education. Dr. Ruth's career took off when she gave a lecture and the talk impressed a manager of WYNY. She offered Ruth twenty-five dollars a week to host "Sexually Speaking," a weekly fifteen-minute show that aired after midnight. It was an immediate success, and Dr. Ruth soon became a household name—leading to multiple radio and television shows and countless pop culture cameos, including Scott Bakula jumping into the body of a 4'7" German woman on *Quantum Leap*.

53

53
THE EAT THE MORONS YEAR

There is conflict all around you—people misbehaving, stealing, abusing Aqua Net—but you're in charge. Don't avoid conflict, dig down deep, pull out your thickest Brooklyn accent, and take no shit. And if anyone has anything to say about it, kick them out of your courtroom. (A bailiff bestie also helps.)

Trust your gut! Make decisions this year and stick to them. Don't let anyone pee on your leg and tell you it's raining. Also, don't let anyone pee on your leg in general. (See entry 64.)

* * *

Judge Judy, born Judith Blum (later Sheindlin), was just a regular gal from a Jewish family in Brooklyn. She earned her bachelor's degree in government from American University and then went on to New York Law School, where she was one of the few female graduates in her class. Initially, Judy worked as a corporate lawyer for a cosmetics company, but she didn't love it, and after taking a break to raise her children, she switched careers to become a prosecutor in the family court system. Then in her forties, she earned a reputation for her no-nonsense attitude, holding sympathy for the wronged, and not taking shit from those who didn't behave. Judy kept climbing and was appointed as a family court judge. In her early fifties, she burst into the national zeitgeist after being profiled by the *Los Angeles Times* and featured on *60 Minutes*. The public loved her, and CBS offered the fifty-three-year-old judge her own show. Judy starred in *The Judge Judy Show* for twenty-five seasons—all with her trusted sidekick, Bailiff Byrd, by her side. She holds the record for not only the longest-running TV courtroom show but also the highest-rated daytime show of all time, with better ratings than even *Oprah*. Yes, OPRAH. A *Reader's Digest* poll of the "100 Most Trusted People in America" revealed the public thought our gal from Brooklyn was the most trustworthy judge, beating all nine U.S. Supreme Court justices.

54

54

THE DON'T CALL ME SHIRLEY YEAR

The plane is going down, and there's only *one* person who can land it. It's not you, but you're *very* supportive.

Surely, you *can* be serious, but being serious all the time is about as much fun as a glass of water to the face. Get yourself a squad who lets you be you. This year explore the absurd, the goofy, the little things that make you laugh. Shoot your shot or just throw your gun instead.

* * *

Leslie Nielsen was a member of the Royal Canadian Air Force during WWII. After the war, he decided to follow in his radio actor uncle's footsteps and study theater at university. He sustained himself with gigs on live local TV shows, which paid only seventy-five dollars, and it wasn't until he was thirty that he landed his first feature flop . . . uh, we mean film. It was *The Vagabond King*, which Nielsen later referred to as *The Vagabond Turkey*. But the producer of the film saw something in him and gave him his first role in a successful movie called *Forbidden Planet*, a sci-fi adaptation of *The Tempest*. For the next two decades, Nielsen always had work but not yet stardom. After bit parts in *Gunsmoke*, *Alfred Hitchcock Presents*, and even the pilot for *Hawaii Five-0*, Nielsen realized he was a handsome leading man in an industry overstocked with handsome leading men. So he started to focus on comedy to stand out. At age fifty-four, he landed (heeey-ooo) the role of Dr. Rumack in *Airplane!* He became known for his deadpan delivery and perfect comedic timing while playing characters oblivious to their absurd surroundings. Nielsen was a new kind of leading man in the *Police Squad!* TV series—which later became the blockbuster *Naked Gun* movie franchise—and earned an Emmy nomination for his comedy chops and habit of throwing guns at criminals.

55

55
THE LIGHT YOUR FIRE YEAR

There are few things scarier in this life than a blank page, but one of those things is someone taking that blank page from you, writing about your world when they've never walked in your shoes. Now is the time to start the fire. Put your fingers on that keyboard, get set up with a narc, learn to make meth, and create a character that makes Nancy Drew look like a million boring white women were taking turns writing her story.

First sentences are hard. Second sentences can be even harder. It might take you a decade, but fire is powerful and so are you.

* * *

Angeline Boulley is a member of the Sault Ste. Marie Tribe of Chippewa Indians located on Sugar Island, between Michigan and Canada. Her father is a traditional firekeeper—a respected position in the tribe, who presides over ceremonies and keeps cultural history alive through storytelling. Her mother was white, making her feel between two worlds as a teen. In high school, her friends tried to set her up with a new handsome guy in school. The date never happened because it was discovered that he was actually an undercover police officer (hate when that happens). The spark of a novel was ignited that year, but it's hard to find time for a creative pursuit. After graduating from Central Michigan University, Boulley went into education, focusing on improving reservation schools at the local and federal levels, working her way up to the role of Director for the Office of Indian Education at the U.S. Department of Education. While she came up with the initial concept for *Firekeeper's Daughter* when she was just eighteen, she didn't start writing until her mid-forties, and it took her ten years to finish. It paid off. The book sparked a bidding war between publishers, and at age fifty-five she saw her book debut at number one on the *New York Times* Best Seller List, gaining huge commercial and critical success.

56

56
THE MODERN YEAR

Life is like a fruit bowl. Covered in oil paint. Wait, let's try that again. Life is two guys playing cards, sold for 259 million dollars. Hmmm. How about this: Life is like a Cézanne painting, worth more than any of those super-famous works that become cliché posters on dorm room walls. Move over *The Scream*. Move over *Sunflowers*. Move over *Velvet Black Light Pot Leaf.*

This year, appreciate the small things. The way light hits an object. The joy of playing a game with friends. The trees. The hills. And, of course, the random human skull next to the food on your table.

* * *

Paul Cézanne began studying art at a young age but turned to law to please his dad. While he pursued his degree, he continued to study painting and drawing on the side. To his father's disappointment, he eventually decided to follow his heart, left law behind, and moved to Paris to focus on art full time. (Parents—they just don't understand!) While in Paris, he met another artist named Pissaro, somehow didn't make fun of his name, and they became fast friends, joining together to develop a Postimpressionist style. The Salon of Paris was not impressed, and Cézanne's works were rejected numerous times and ridiculed by art critics who were still all about the Impressionists. It took years for the world to realize Cézanne was ahead of his time. When he was fifty-six, he was given his first solo exhibit and his work was finally recognized for its brilliance. Cézanne may not have been appreciated by critics of the time, but he was considered a master by up-and-coming artists like Matisse and Picasso, who called him the "Father of Us All." And this father was much more supportive of taking risks and forging your own way.

57

57

THE BE THE BADDIE YEAR

Sure, it's fun to be hanging in a group of your childhood friends, running around, having adventures, finding dead bodies so old they're just comical skeletons in snazzy outfits . . . but have you tried being THE VILLAIN Rules? Pah! You don't need those. You *make* the rules, often while surrounded by minions sporting thick fake accents and the desire to make all your wicked dreams a reality!

Embrace your bad side this year. Follow what makes you happy! Rewrite the rules! Kidnap random children!

Okay . . . maybe not that last one but definitely the others.

* * *

Anne Ramsey was born in Nebraska, the daughter of the National Treasurer of the Girl Scouts of America. You'd think she'd become famous for being a model citizen, but Ramsay found a more entertaining role: playing the baddie. Ramsey first became interested in acting while attending Bennington College in Vermont. After graduation, she acted on the stage for a few decades, working her way up to Broadway. But Ramsey set her sights on a wider audience and started to land bit roles in TV and movies, parts so small she was almost always uncredited. Hollywood shoved her into roles like "Lady with Cat," "Spinster #2," and "Wife of Crazy Man." But no one was going to hold Mama Fratelli back, and Ramsey stole the show with her performance as the criminal master-mom in the cult classic *The Goonies*, winning herself a Saturn Award—her first acting honor—at age fifty-seven. Two years later, she got her second Saturn Award for *Throw Momma from the Train*, but this role also came with Oscar and Golden Globe nominations. Sometimes being bad can be very, very good.

58

THE GET THAT WINDMILL YEAR

Do you hate architecture? Green energy? Things that spin? Have we got the career path for you!

We all see our giants in different ways. Towering over us. Making us doubt our talents. If you believe something, don't give up. You've got great friends and a great ass. Those windmills don't stand a chance.

* * *

Miguel de Cervantes spent his life largely in poverty and obscurity. When he was still a child, his family was forced to leave Spain for Rome. Cervantes joined the military and was severely wounded in battle. Things didn't get much better as soon after, he was captured by pirates and held captive for five years. He was eventually ransomed, rescued by missionaries, and returned to Spain, where he became a tax collector, writing unsuccessful plays on the side. When he was thirty-eight, he published his first novel, *La Galatea*, but it garnered little attention. Twenty years later, at age fifty-eight, he finally made it big when he published his masterwork, *Don Quixote*, about the adventures of a delusional "knight," his companion, and their donkey. The book is considered the first modern novel, and it was groundbreaking for upending the chivalric romantic form of literature that had been popular for more than a century and for featuring realistic scenarios and everyday speech in a literary context. *Don Quixote* has been translated into seventy languages and boasts over eleven-hundred editions worldwide.

59

59
THE LANDMARK YEAR

Not all heroes wear capes. Some wear robes. There are laws all around us. There's that whole gravity thing and the "objects in motion stay in motion" thing, but it's the laws we've created as humans that can truly weigh us down.

This is your year to fight for those around you. To notice when a neighbor or a friend or a whole group of people isn't being treated right. Laws were meant to be . . . well, not *broken* (hi, law enforcement reading this!) . . . but definitely questioned. We've defied gravity, and maybe your robe is less Supreme and more "polka-dot terrycloth," but you can still change the world in it.

* * *

Thurgood Marshall grew up in a family where dinner entertainment was his father rehashing the legal arguments he had witnessed at the local courthouse, which he attended for fun. The stories enthralled a young Thurgood. Determined to become a lawyer, Marshall wanted to attend the University of Maryland School of Law, but they didn't accept Black students. He went on to study law at Howard University. After graduation, he tried to start his own law practice but again faced discrimination. So he worked with the NAACP, and, as fate would have it, one of his first cases was against the University of Maryland School of Law on behalf of another well-qualified Black candidate who was rejected. Marshall won. He joined the NAACP officially and went on to successfully argue a series of cases that went before the Supreme Court, including 1954's *Brown v. Board of Education of Topeka*, which directly challenged the constitutionality of *Plessy v. Ferguson* and the basis of all "separate but equal" laws. This case was a landmark decision for the American Civil Rights Movement and Marshall was soon after appointed as a court of appeals judge, then solicitor general of the United States, and finally justice of the Supreme Court at the age of fifty-nine, becoming the first Black man to hold a seat on the highest court in the country.

60

60

THE NO REGRETS YEAR

When life gives you divorce, make divorce-ade.

What do you do when it feels like your world is falling apart? Make a new world! A whole new world! A whole new Disney World even! Or better yet, start putting yourself out there. And who knows, you may wind up the President . . . 's secretary.

Leave those weak relationships in your past and focus on your future. You've got this.

* * *

Kathryn Joosten was born in 1939 in Chicago and followed the general path expected of most women of her time: become a nurse (in her case, a psychiatric one), get married, and pop out a couple of kids. But when she was in her early forties, two things happened—her marriage fell apart and her mother died. In the late stages of her illness, Kathryn's mother confided in her many regrets, things she always wanted to do that she never took the steps to achieve. Joosten vowed to follow her heart and dreams from then on. She began acting in community theater at the age of forty-two. When she was fifty-three years old, she got a job as a street performer at Disney World, working alongside actors decades younger than her. But her goal was TV, and she moved to Hollywood and started to land bit parts on shows. When Joosten was sixty, she landed her first recurring role, the incomparable Mrs. Landingham on the smash hit series *The West Wing*. She went on to other regular roles, winning two Emmys for her turn as the acidic Karen McCluskey in *Desperate Housewives.*

61

61

THE DENCH, JUDI DENCH YEAR

You're a big fish in a pretty decent-sized pond. You've won all the fish awards and become a pond-hold name, respected and admired by every fish in the vicinity. But have you seen that pond over *there*?! That one's practically an *ocean*.

Don't let comfort hold you back. Why be a household name in one country when you can be one all over the planet?

* * *

Dame Judi Dench loved the theater from a very young age and studied acting in college. She made her stage debut in *Hamlet* at age twenty-two and continued to work mostly in theater for the next twenty-five years, taking on every leading female Shakespeare role in addition to some comedic and musical work and earning several BAFTAs while she was at it. Dench was widely known in her native England but not as well-known beyond. She earned minor recognition as the star of the TV romantic comedy *As Time Goes By*, but it was her role in the blockbuster James Bond film *GoldenEye* that introduced her—at age sixty-one—to an international audience. And hot damn! Finally, the Bond Girl we've deserved all this time! She hasn't stopped since.

62

62
THE PUT A RING ON IT YEAR

You're comfortable. You know all your neighbors. You have an amazing best friend who would follow you to the ends of the earth and an uncle who only occasionally turns invisible and tries to bite you over family heirlooms. But there's something you're missing. Maybe it's a wizard, a dwarf, two charming-yet-plot-advancing hobbits, and a white dude, and another white dude, and a third white dude, but this one has, like, pointy ears or something.

This year, join together with friends. Combine efforts to make the world just a little bit brighter. And remember that small things add up: a single sentence written a day, an hour volunteering, or donating just one of your fingers—and a creature named Gollum—to the fires of Mount Doom.

Just don't forget about second breakfast.

* * *

J. R. R. Tolkien, or John Ronald Reuel Tolkien, was born in South Africa. He was orphaned at a young age, raised partially by relatives and then a Catholic priest who became his guardian. He earned a degree from Exeter College, specializing in literature and Anglo-Saxon and Germanic languages, became a lieutenant in WWI, and, after the war, finally began his career as a college professor at Oxford. There, he started a writing group called the Inklings with friends, including some dude named C. S. Lewis. (Is the key to being an amazing writer not telling anyone your first and middle names?) When he was forty-five, Tolkien published his first book, *The Hobbit*. It was well-received, but it was considered a children's book and looked down on by snooty people. He focused the next decade of his life on writing his opus, *The Lord of the Rings* trilogy. The first book in the series, *The Fellowship of the Ring*, was published when he was sixty-two and became a global bestseller, inspiring a blockbuster movie franchise and leading to your friend's terrible Gollum impression.

63

THE GOLDEN YEAR

Picture it. Your sixty-third birthday. Your wit is sharp. Your sequins gleam. You steal every single scene.

Say what you're thinking. Don't hold back. Take a trip to Florida. Grab a slice of cheesecake with a loved one and her eccentric, pastel-wearing friends.

* * *

Estelle Getty had a New York City childhood filled with entertainment. Her father would take the family to see a movie and a vaudeville show every Friday night. Getty was hooked and became determined to find her way to an acting career. She graduated from high school and took a job as a secretary, going to theater auditions in the evenings. But nothing ever quite took off. When she was nearly sixty years old, with the help of a friend, she got her first big role on the stage. Thank YOU for being a friend, Harvey Fierstein. He created the role of Mrs. Beckoff in *Torch Song Trilogy* specifically for Getty. She received a Drama Desk nomination, and it led her to audition for the role that would define her acting career. At age sixty-three, Getty gained recognition as the feisty, wise-cracking Sophia Petrillo—the most golden of *The Golden Girls*—when the show took home an Emmy and a Golden Globe for its first season.

64

64

THE TAKE THAT, JELLYFISH YEAR

People say that life is putting one foot in front of the other, but sometimes it's more about putting one arm in front of the other . . . while kicking furiously and hoping a jellyfish doesn't get ya right in the face.

Make a goal and keep it! It may take years. It may take decades, but you're strong, determined. The water that's challenging you is also inside of you. Like a lot of it. Something like 75% of you is water. Embrace it and conquer it.

And if you should happen to get stung, don't let anyone pee on you.

(Seriously, it doesn't work. Who started this urban legend?! Wait, don't tell us. We don't want to know.)

* * *

Diana Nyad began swimming competitively in the seventh grade. She was a natural. Nyad won three Florida state championships and hoped to compete in the Olympics, but she was unable to due to a heart infection. She began marathon swimming in college and set a world record in her first ten-mile race. She started doing stunts like swimming the twenty-eight miles around Manhattan and not growing an extra limb from the pollution. When she was thirty, she swam from the Bahamas to Florida, setting a record that still stands today—and all that without a wetsuit. That same year, she decided to try to swim from Cuba to Key West. It was the first time water got the better of her. The attempt was unsuccessful, and she spent the next thirty-plus years determined to complete the route. Multiple jellyfish stings, currents pushing her off course . . . it seemed like she had finally met her match. But she didn't give up, and at age sixty-four Nyad finally conquered her goal by swimming the 110 miles from Cuba to Florida in fifty-three hours.

65

65

THE DEEP-FRIED YEAR

You've been marinating for a while, but now you're ready to spice up any party. It's okay to keep some secrets this year, but it's also okay to share those secrets with your franchised locations. Spread love and deep-fried breading and the world will take notice.

Something this tasty isn't just born. You're seasoned to perfection and best served with a side of buttery cornbread.

* * *

Colonel Sanders was born Harland Sanders in 1890 in Indiana. His father died when Harland was just six years old, and his mother had to get a job, leaving Harland in charge of feeding and caring for his younger siblings. He took to cooking very easily but never thought of it as a career. Instead, he worked as a farmer, army wagoner, streetcar conductor, railroad fireman, ferry boat captain, and tire salesman. (More like tired salesman. Yeesh!) Known among friends for his fried chicken, at forty—at this point he was running a gas service station—he started to sell his signature dish out of his home. People went mad for it, and within five years he had made enough to take over a restaurant. He perfected his secret recipe, and it became so popular that he was named a "Colonel" by the state of Kentucky. At age sixty-five, Sanders tried his hand at tickling the taste buds of the rest of the country . . . and soon after, the world. He launched a successful chain that became one of the first fast-food restaurants to expand internationally. In less than ten years, Kentucky Fried Chicken had more than six-hundred locations, and Colonel Sanders became an international icon, portrayed by such greats as Norm MacDonald and even Mario Lopez in a sexy Lifetime movie. That's a whole lotta spice!

66

66

THE VAXX'ED TO THE MAXX YEAR

Do you like airplanes? Science! Do you like lasers? Science! Do you like cures for diseases? Science! Do you like when you accidentally drag your feet on a carpet and then shock yourself on a doorknob? Ouch! (Also: Science!)

Science is a team sport, a collaboration of minds; but sometimes there's an MVP, a Jordan waiting to fly. (Though, disclaimer, he can't actually fly. Science!) Use this year to appreciate all the advances we've made. The working toilet. The heaters that keep you warm and air-conditioning that keeps you cool. And your absolute lack of polio.

* * *

Katalin "Kati" Karikó grew up in a small village in Hungary. She loved science from an early age and went on get her PhD from the University of Szeged. There she began her postdoctoral research into mRNA—a type of single-stranded RNA involved in protein synthesis with implications for viral and immunotherapies. But sadly, her funding ran out in Hungary, and she made the hard choice to move to the U.S. with her family to continue her research. She believed in her research and that mRNA was the key to unlocking several thorny medical problems, but her work was widely dismissed and overlooked by other scientists and scientific journals. For nearly ten years, she chased grants and funding, struggling to stay afloat in academia. She began to doubt herself and the potential of mRNA. But the world needed Karikó, and she found a new collaborator, Dr. Drew Weissman. He shared a passion for the potential of mRNA, and together they finally had a breakthrough. Their research was later instrumental in the development of the COVID-19 vaccine.

67

THE MABLEY IT'S TIME YEAR

There's a spotlight waiting for you, a mic in the center and at the ready. People will try to give you a list—a list of reasons why it isn't your light—but you know better. Put on your comfiest housedress and slippers because glass ceilings don't need to be broken with uncomfortable heels. They're broken with sharp minds and tongues.

You've always been amazing. It's time the world started to take notice.

Also, do you know how many gold records you can fit in a baggy housedress?

* * *

Jackie "Moms" Mabley was born Loretta Mary Aiken in 1894, and to say she had a traumatic childhood is an understatement. At the age of fourteen, her grandmother encouraged her to run away and join a vaudeville show. Around this time, she took the stage name Jackie Mabley, and she quickly became one the most successful performers on the segregated "Chitlin' Circuit." Her fanbase continued to grow, and for the next thirty years, she played the Apollo stage more than any other performer, earning up to ten-thousand dollars a week. But she was still only known to the Black community. In her fifties, she created her "Moms" character, embracing the maternal role she often had with younger performers on the circuit. The non-threatening persona of a frumpy old woman (with a penchant for younger men) allowed her to address taboo subjects like racism and sexuality in a way that was palatable to audiences. While she was never fully out to the public, she was very open with friends and family that she was queer. The 1950s and '60s were hard times to be a female comedian—but to be a Black, LGBTQ comedian? Almost impossible. But Mabley was a fighter in a housedress, tearing down walls for those who followed her. At the age of sixty-seven, she earned her first gold record for the album *The Funniest Woman in the World*, going on to appear on several TV shows, like *The Ed Sullivan Show*, and perform at Carnegie Hall at age sixty-eight.

68

68

THE SUPER SPEED YEAR

What's got two wheels and an intense Doppler Effect?
Two unicyclists falling down a hill.

Also, a motorcyclist going *very* fast.

Sure, you could be like your neighbors, buying fancy new convertibles to keep up with the Joneses. But how about instead you keep working on the vehicle you have? Put all your love into it. Make it better as time goes by.

So get on that bike—or whatever your dream is—and ride.

* * *

Herbert James "Burt" Munro developed an interest in speed at an early age. He would ride horses as fast as he could across the family farm, much to his parents' chagrin. Munro worked in construction and then found work as a motorcycle mechanic and salesman. It was only a matter of time before he would test his speed again. His first motorcycle, an Indian Scout, had a top speed of 55 miles per hour, but that wasn't enough for Munro's taste, so he began to tinker and make modifications. Not having much money, he fashioned his own parts by casting from recycled materials and often made his own tools too. He rose to the top of the New Zealand motorcycle scene, but he wanted the international challenge. When he was sixty-three years old, he traveled to the Bonneville Salt Flats in Utah to attempt speed records. There he went on to set three world records, including, at age sixty-eight, a top speed of 184.087 miles per hour—a record that still stands today—on the original bike he had nurtured over the years.

69

69
THE SHUFFLE IT UP YEAR

Can we interest you in a game of poker? Or maybe you'd prefer rummy, hearts, blackjack, cribbage, solitaire, euchre, spades, or 52-card pickup. (If you are a younger sibling, you definitely know that last one.)

If you ever think you've run out of possibilities—that all the pieces of you are just made for one thing—think of a deck of cards. With just fifty-two cards there are hundreds of thousands of possibilities. We have eighty-six billion neurons and thirty trillion cells inside of us. Just think of the possibilities we contain.

* * *

Edmond Hoyle was born in the late 1600s and little is known about his early life. A lover of cards, in his late sixties, he found his way into high-society parlors—a social scene filled with rich people eager to learn the card games he taught. For his pupils, he wrote down his notes in a collection he called *A Short Treatise on the Game of Whist*. The demand for his book grew, which lead Hoyle to publish it, sharing his card game knowledge with a wider audience. He went on to write the rules for backgammon, piquet, chess, and quadrille. He is considered the first technical game writer, and the phrase "According to Hoyle" is still used today—shorthand for "strictly according to the rules."

70

70
THE ETYMOLOGY YEAR

What defines old age?
Nothing does. Especially before the dictionary was invented. Heeeey-oooo!

* * *

Noah Webster was a curious kid who loved to learn. Though not many people went to college in the eighteenth century, his parents were able to send him to Yale to study at the age of sixteen. There were a few interruptions to his studies though, namely the American Revolution, and when he graduated and hoped to continue on to law school, his parents no longer had the money to support him. So Webster paid his own way doing clerical work and teaching, studied law at night, and eventually passed the bar on his own. While he was a student and later a teacher, Webster found that American educational texts were in need of updating. This led him to publish his own textbook, *A Grammatical Institute of the English Language*, which was widely adopted and used to teach American children to read, spell, and pronounce words for over a hundred years. When Webster was in his mid-forties, he began compiling and defining the words that Americans used, many of which had previously not been documented. His first collection contained about thirty-seven thousand words and their brief definitions. It was the first of its kind. He continued to work on his collection for twenty-two years, and when he was seventy, he finally published it as the *American Dictionary of the English Language*. Webster's dictionary is still widely used today.

71

71

THE ROLL WITH IT YEAR

Rivers are a lot like life: winding in strange ways, suffering from low points at times, and often with more bumps than you'd like. But rivers are masters at taking those sharp rocks and letting them know who's boss. It may take decades, but any rock can be smoothed, just like most obstacles.

Discover a new mode of travel this year. Maybe it's finding a new hiking trail, learning to ride a motorcycle, or captaining the itty-bittiest of boats. The water may not always be smooth, but it's no match for you.

* * *

Edward "Ed" Earle was always athletic, running track and playing soccer through high school and college. However, it wasn't until Earle was forty that he turned his racing ambitions to the water. His start in this new sport began by chance. He wanted to buy a sailboat to sail with his son, but it was too expensive, so he instead bought a canoe, and they started racing together. His son's interest waned, but Earle's interest grew, and he switched over to sea kayaking, competing in his first nationals when he was fifty. For Earle, kayaking was serious business, and he dedicated himself to training, hitting the gym and/or water five to six days a week. All that dedication paid off. Earle routinely beat competitors who were thirty or forty years younger than him, holding several kayak course race records throughout New England and winning the Run of the Charles Open Kayak and Canoe Race for three straight years, starting at age seventy. And he beat his own record at the age of seventy-one and again at age seventy-two.

72
THE CIRCUMNAVIGATE YEAR

It's time to take a trip. Get away from your daily life. View the world from a different angle. Fly west! Keep going! Past continents, past oceans. You're so far away from home, farther than you've ever . . . oh wait, you're back. Forgot about that whole "round earth" thing.

The globe is your oyster, but, like, only metaphorically. Please don't try to eat a globe, you'll only get Australia in your teeth. Explore, keep moving, and remember life isn't a race . . . but if it was, you'd totally win.

* * *

Margaret Ringenberg discovered her love of the sky when, at seven years old, she saw a barnstormer land near her parents' house, and he gave her an airplane ride. She earned her pilot's license and completed her first solo flight when she was just nineteen. During WWII, she flew with the WASPs—a noncombat group made up of more than a thousand highly skilled, kick-ass female pilots. After the war, she became a commercial pilot and flight instructor, but she wanted to race as well, something women at the time just didn't do. Ringenberg competed in over 150 air races over the course of her life and capped off her prolific flight career by completing the around-the-world race at the age of seventy-two.

73

73

THE ANNUAL ANNUM YEARLY YEAR

Greet this year with joy, jubilation, jollity, and jocundity.

And if that doesn't work you should try some glee, enchantment, pleasure, mirth, delectation, blissfulness, beatitude, felicity, and delight.

Just don't give in to anxiety, agita, anxiousness, apprehension, agitation, or aardvarks. Those guys don't even know how thesauruses work.

* * *

Peter Mark Roget was an eighteenth-century physician and lecturer who practiced medicine until he retired at sixty-one. Throughout his life Roget suffered from depression, but he discovered that if he wrote down lists of words, it helped him through his bouts of sadness. He found comfort in naming as many words that meant the same thing as he could. By the time of his retirement, Roget had compiled some fifteen thousand synonyms. He worked on his thesaurus for twelve more years until it was published when he was seventy-three. The first edition of the thesaurus was fantastically titled, *Thesaurus of English Words and Phrases Classified and Arranged So as to Facilitate the Expression of Ideas and Assist in Literary Composition*, and it became a staple in the homes of the English-speaking world (though with the much shorter, and more boring, title of *Roget's Thesaurus*).

74

74
THE WATERSHED YEAR

It's easy to put others before yourself. Maybe it's your kids, the students you teach, or your older brother who *definitely* ought to be played by Brad Pitt in the movie version of your life.

Put yourself first this year. Do the things you've pushed to the side. Don't follow the path everyone else follows. Take up fly-fishing. Befriend a lumberjack. Write that novella. Or two or three.

But only publish two of them and skip that third one you called "Logging and Pimping." Seriously.

* * *

Norman Maclean's early education was provided by his father, a reverend. He had a lifelong love of writing and literature and was always telling stories. At Dartmouth College he became the editor of their humor magazine and went on to a master's degree, then a doctorate in English literature from the University of Chicago. Maclean took the English major's river-most-traveled and taught, becoming a professor of Romantic poetry and Shakespeare. He retired from teaching at age seventy-one and was encouraged by his family to write down the stories he would tell. Those stories became *A River Runs Through It and Other Stories*, published when Maclean was seventy-four: a collection of three novellas about his life growing up in Montana. It was published to widespread acclaim, and the titular story was turned into a beloved movie starring Sir Pitt. Inexplicably, some of the other novellas in the book, like "Logging and Pimping" and "Your Pal, Jim," did not get made into films.

75

75
THE MAUDE YEAR

If you want to sing out, sing out.
And if you want to be free, be free.

Perhaps this is the year to take a younger friend under your wing. Show them all the amazing things you've learned in this world, like how to steal both cars and hearts. Do exactly what you want and don't listen to what the world has to say about it. You're smart, you're free, and you're damn sexy.

* * *

Ruth Gordon was a prolific actress, playwright, screenwriter, and memoirist. From an early age, Gordon was committed to becoming an actress; so committed, in fact, that when she was in her early twenties she had both of her legs broken and reset to correct her bow-leggedness. (Uh, whaaaa?) With her newly straightened legs, she went on to do silent films, Broadway, and eventually talkies. When Ruth was in her mid-forties, she added writing to her repertoire, penning several notable screenplays with her husband as well as stage plays and a three-volume memoir. As she got up in years, Gordon played many notable supporting roles, including the villainous neighbor in *Rosemary's Baby*, for which she won an Oscar. But it was her role as the outgoing octogenarian who has an affair with an introverted twenty-something in the film *Harold and Maude* that solidified her stardom. While the movie was initially a commercial flop, it is one of the first films to be considered a cult classic and is still widely adored.

76

76

THE EMPEROR OF ICE CREAM YEAR

Call the owner of big words,
The literary one, and bid you write,
The best emperor is the emperor of dreams.

This might be your year to embrace a pen, a computer, a 1922 Model 1 Remington Portable. You've got words. Share them.

And we know the poem isn't *actually* about ice cream, but maybe use this as an excuse to eat ice cream whenever you feel like it this year. If you feel bloated after, maybe that's just poetry trying to get out.

* * *

Wallace Stevens was not exactly a person you'd expect to write poetry. He was educated at Harvard and then New York Law School and largely worked in insurance during his career. But secretly, around age thirty-five, he began dabbling in poetry and even published infrequently under a pseudonym. A businessman by day and a poet by night, his first collection was quietly released when he was forty-four, but it wasn't until his seventies that he began to get recognition. He took home two National Book Awards, one at age seventy-two for *The Auroras of Autumn* and the second at age seventy-six for *The Collected Poems of Wallace Stevens*, for which he also won the Pulitzer Prize and which is still considered one of the greatest poetry volumes of all time.

77
THE READY PLAYER 001 YEAR

A good chunk of your life is spent with people telling you to grow up, stop playing games. But what if playing those games could lower your stress, heighten the connectivity of your synapses, and help you avoid getting shot by a giant animatronic schoolgirl?

This is the year to revisit something you loved when you were fresh to the world. It could be a playground game, a picture book, a K-drama turned international phenomenon, or even your first friends, because friends are who are going to get you through this Netflix original . . . uh, I mean life.

* * *

O Yeong-su had a tumultuous childhood growing up near the thirty-eighth parallel during the Korean War. His father was killed and his brother was kidnapped by North Korea during the conflict. Unsurprisingly, O Yeong-su meandered a bit in his early life until he found his way to the theater. Initially, he worked behind the scenes, but acting was his true calling. Most of his career was spent as part of the National Theater of Korea, where he tackled roles in classic plays by the likes of Shakespeare, Faulkner, and Camus. Through the course of his lengthy career, O Yeong-su acted in more than two hundred stage productions and landed small roles in television and movies, though he remained largely unknown even in his native Korea. After acting for more than fifty years, O Yeong-Su "Red Light, Green Light"-ed onto the global stage with his portrayal of Oh Il-nam in the Netflix series *Squid Game* and made history by becoming the first South Korean to win a Golden Globe.

78

78

THE CHANGE UP YEAR

Everyone knows that to be a true artist you need beautifully stretched, acid-free archival canvas, hundreds of the highest quality oil paints, hand-made natural-hair brushes, an ergonomic floor mat to help with hip alignment, and a perfectly placed window so that the sunlight can cascade through, showcasing every brush stroke. Or maybe you just need some house paint, fireboards, and a desire to say, "F everything you think Grandmas ought to be doing!"

Don't let anyone box you in for your gender or your age or the fact you always thought sewing was super boring. This year, create something that makes you happy. Find your medium and share it with the world.

* * *

Grandma Moses, born Anna Mary Robertson, left home at a young age to work on a farm. While she was interested in art as a child, the demands of farm life left her little opportunity to explore her curiosity. She married and gave birth to ten children, only five of whom survived infancy. Moses worked on the family farm with her husband and children, earning additional money by selling homemade goods and food. She didn't care for traditional pastimes like knitting or sewing, but she did make needlework pictures and quilts, often portraying bucolic scenes of farm life. At age seventy-eight, when arthritis rendered her unable to continue embroidery, she took up painting. Initially, she used whatever materials she could find: house paint, leftover canvas, and fireboards. In 1939, at age seventy-nine, three of her paintings were included in an exhibit at the Metropolitan Museum of Art called *Contemporary Unknown American Painters*, launching Moses into the public consciousness. At age eighty, she received her first solo exhibit titled *What a Farm Wife Painted*. She continued to exhibit worldwide through her nineties and painted until a few months before her death at age 101.

79

79
THE KING ME YEAR

You're a Queen, and while everyone around you can move in only one general direction, you have free will, free movement, and the board is yours to explore. What? There's no Queen in checkers? Okay, fine, then you're the little horsie. Just when your enemies think you are moving their way, you turn sharply, making cute horsie L-shapes . . . no horses either?

Perhaps this is the year to pick the unconventional choice. Follow that Robert Frost overgrown path no one is taking (but wear long pants and check for ticks after). If the world obsesses over chess—from TV shows to movies to televised tournaments—you can choose to play checkers, because life should be more like checkers: joyfully hopping over obstacles in your way.

* * *

Asa Long loved checkers from birth—well maybe not birth, but definitely shortly after. He became the youngest person to ever win the U.S. National Checkers Championship at age eighteen. Long then went on to win the World Checkers Championship when he was thirty. Though he played consistently his whole life, he became less competitive over the years, losing several tournaments. Don't call it a comeback (though it was totally a comeback), but when he was in his late seventies, he won the national championship again, beating players one third of his age. Long now holds the titles for both the oldest (seventy-nine) and youngest (eighteen) person to win the National Checkers Championship.

80

80
THE SAY, "GOODNIGHT" YEAR

People fear never achieving their dreams, but what if you achieved them young? What if the best thing you ever did was catch that winning football when you were eighteen, make that highly realistic dried macaroni Abe Lincoln at five, or what if you made the world laugh for decades alongside your soulmate/comedy partner, until suddenly you found yourself alone, smoking piles of cigars, with no one to listen to your jokes?

It's never too late to start again! Maybe it's something new, but perhaps it's rekindling your prior love of comedy or acting or pasta portraiture. Only you get to decide when to say, "Goodnight, Gracie."

* * *

George Burns was born Nathan Birnbaum and was the ninth of twelve kids. His father died when Burns was seven, and he had to help support the family, working as an errand boy, shoeshine boy, and syrup maker. Burns would often sing to pass the time, and he formed a group called the Pee-Wee Quartet. They performed in saloons, on ferries, and in brothels. He took up smoking his trademark cigars when he was only fourteen years old. Things came together when he met the love of his life, Gracie Allen. They started a radio show, which ran for nearly seventeen years, before they transformed it into the TV program, *The George Burns and Gracie Allen Show*. It ran for eight seasons, but when Allen decided to step away from the spotlight, it was canceled. Burns went on to tour, but nothing captured audiences like when he was with Gracie. Sadly, she died when he was sixty-eight, and he quit acting. Ten years later, he was cast in *The Sunshine Boys*, replacing his late friend, Jack Benny. It was this role that brought Burns back, and it also won him an Oscar at the age of eighty. Burns went on to star in several other hit movies—and smoke an unfathomable amount of cigars—until his death, shortly after he turned one hundred.

81

81

THE WHERE'S THE BEEF YEAR

What's the beef? How's the beef? Why's the beef? When's the beef? Who's the beef? Beef's the beef? Beef.

The world owes you the beef. Somewhere the beef is hiding, waiting for you (but, like, not in a creepy way, in a cool beef way). Find that beef. Conquer that beef. Don't settle for less.

* * *

Clara Peller immigrated to Chicago from Russia as a child and spent thirty-five years working as a manicurist at a local salon. When she was eighty years old, she was hired to portray a . . . manicurist in a TV commercial (a role she had unknowingly been working toward her whole life!). The ad agency admired her no-nonsense attitude and unique voice, and they started to give her more commercial work. At age eighty-one, Peller got her first big break in a Massachusetts state lottery commercial, which led to her role as the Wendy's "Where's the Beef?" lady. Her perfect delivery of the three-word tagline made her an instant cultural hit and national icon. The restaurant chain's annual revenue rose nearly 31% that year, and Peller's snarky catchphrase captured the hearts of America.

82

THE PICK THINGS UP AND PUT THEM DOWN YEAR

There are dangers lurking everywhere. The world is not a safe place. Like when you're a burglar, but your mark winds up being the strongest eighty-year-old in the world and completely kicks your ass. Like not just a little bit. Like a "repeatedly being hit with a table until the table itself breaks" level of ass-kicking.

Find your strength this year. Embrace that our bodies have an amazing ability to adapt and grow. And maybe don't break into the house of a champion powerlifter.

* * *

Willie Murphy spent over forty years of her life working for the New York state government. She took up track at the age of fifty, and to better train for her races, she started to lift weights at age seventy-four. She soon discovered that she loved lifting and how strong it made her feel. From that point on, she worked out nearly every day, doing casual one-handed push-ups and deadlifting twice her body weight. She won a World Natural Powerlifting Federation of the Year award, and they even had to create a new category for her because she had aged out of all the ones they had. But it was a chance encounter that brought her the broader national spotlight. One night, eighty-two-year-old Willie was minding her own business at home when a man broke in. He was in for an unpleasant surprise when she picked up the nearest object to defend herself, which happened to be a large table, and hit him with it until it broke. She then proceeded to jump on him and dump a bottle of shampoo on him. The intruder was yelling for an ambulance by the time the police arrived. Murphy didn't press charges, knowing the would-be thief had learned his lesson. Never underestimate an eighty-two-year-old woman.

83

THE SPIN ME 'ROUND YEAR

How many sparkles are you wearing right now? Hint, the answer is NOT ENOUGH. Put on your best bedazzled vest, don your favorite glittery cap, and get down to business. What's the sense in getting older if you can't be the shimmering center of attention? Be a human disco ball with the world dancing around you.

Hit that cross-fade, don't let the beat drop, and make your own party. Vibe to your own rhythm and don't be afraid to mix it up.

* * *

DJ Sumirock, known most of her life as Sumiko Iwamura, grew up dreaming of traveling abroad, but she quickly got pulled into working at her family's restaurant. Her father was previously a jazz drummer and discouraged Sumirock from pursuing music in any form. She got work as a chef and went on to inherit her family's restaurant, where she continues to cook. When she was seventy-seven, she decided to take a class at a DJ school, thinking it would be amusing. What she didn't expect was to completely fall in love. At eighty-three, DJ Sumirock, with her sparkly costumes and personality, was recognized as the world's oldest professional DJ.

84

84

THE RARE BIRD YEAR

Sure, maybe you've thought about *making* art, but have you ever considered *becoming* art? You start each day a blank canvas. Most of us just throw on some paint (or pants on a good day), but there are rare birds among us who delight in the visual puzzle where style and function join hands and, like, totally make out.

Up your fashion game. Treat yourself to a beautiful garment even if you don't think you have an occasion to wear it. *You* are the occasion. Rearrange your space and surround yourself with beauty. And if you happen to wear glasses, don't hide them. Get yourself the biggest pair you can find and demand the world pay attention.

* * *

Iris Apfel grew up traveling from her home in Queens to Manhattan to explore. With an eye for antiques and oddities, she began collecting, and these trips were the foundation for what would become her enormous jewelry collection. She studied art education in college, and her career bounced around—from a copywriter for *Women's Wear Daily* to an illustrator's assistant and finally to an interior designer. She married and, together with her husband, Carl, started a successful textile company focused on replicating vintage European fabrics. When she was eighty-four, The Costume Institute at The Metropolitan Museum of Art premiered an exhibit of statement-glasses-wearing Apfel and her style. They called it *Rara Avis: Selections from the Iris Barrel Apfel Collection*. It was the museum's first time dedicating a full fashion exhibit to a living person who wasn't a designer, and the show brought Apfel's incomparable style to the masses.

85

85

THE GAMER GRANDMA YEAR

You're no noob, so you know that this wide world always has something to explore, be it a cave, a dungeon, a vast wilderness, or the fantastical experience of being murdered by a chicken. Don't be an NPC who just gives others quests. Accept your own missions and take on any monsters that cross your path.

This might be your year to try a new way to play. It could be a board game, a videogame, or competitive quilting. You never know how many friends you might gain.

* * *

Skyrim Grandma, real name Shirley Curry, stumbled into playing videogames when she was in her early sixties and had received a computer from her son that had a copy of *Civilization II* on it. She never expected to get into gaming; she had only wanted the computer to organize her collection of recipes. But playing videogames made her very happy, so she joined YouTube to watch other gamers and eventually got the courage to begin uploading her own streaming gameplay. Fellow gamers fell in love. Curry's wholesome, kind demeanor and open heart made her streams stand out. She would sweetly narrate the games as she played, a big favorite of hers being *Skyrim*—a rather serious action game in which, yes, you can be killed by a chicken. Curry has been called the Bob Ross of video games as her soothing narration has been known to put watchers into a Zen-like state. She lovingly calls her followers her Grandkids—all one million of them. Before discovering gaming, Curry was a member of her local quilting guild and spent most of her time reading. The *New York Times* wrote an article on Skyrim Grandma and her fans, and at age eighty-five, she became immortalized as an NPC in a *Skyrim* game.

86

86

THE BETWEEN TWO WORLDS YEAR

You've already lived through so much. You need to document it because no two eyes in the world have seen exactly the same things as yours. Well maybe *two* eyes have but probably not three and definitely not four.

Tell your stories, find your medium. Maybe it's a fancy, leather-bound journal. And maybe it's fifteen hundred scraps of cardboard. Don't let circumstances you can't control get in the way. Believe in yourself and in your voice. You never know what you'll inspire.

* * *

William "Bill" Traylor was a Black man born enslaved in Alabama. He lived through some of the most tumultuous times in American history: the Civil War, Emancipation, Reconstruction, and Jim Crow segregation. Traylor spent his adult life working as a sharecropper until he moved to Montgomery when he was in his mid-seventies. Sadly, he struggled to make ends meet and found himself unhoused. He would spend his days sitting on the street, a fixture in the Monroe Street neighborhood. One day he picked up a pencil and a scrap of cardboard and began documenting his memories and observations. Over the next three years, he created nearly fifteen hundred pieces of art. His artwork was discovered when he was eighty-six, leading to his first, and only, gallery exhibit at the age of eighty-seven. Though he didn't achieve much notoriety in his lifetime, today Bill Traylor's art is considered a visually striking distillation of his life and experiences, and he is now recognized as a significant figure in American folk art.

87

87

THE DANCING QUEEN YEAR

March with legends like Gandhi and MLK? Sure! Achieve the incredibly difficult yoga "lifting lotus" pose? Easy! Become a successful Hollywood actress? Check. Take down systems of oppression while being a wine connoisseur? Obviously.

You've already lived more lives than most and are fierce at your core. But there's a time to fight and there's a time to dance. This year is a time to dance. Befriend someone one-fourth your age and connect through movement. Prove to yourself, and everyone else, that it's never too late to try something totally new and maybe rack up a few hundred trophies while you're at it.

* * *

Tao Porchon-Lynch is the embodiment of *joie de vivre*. Over the course of her lifetime, she was many things: resistance fighter, cabaret dancer, couture model, actress, film producer, international film distributor, wine enthusiast, yoga instructor, and ballroom dancer. Lynch began her life dramatically, born on a ship in the middle of the English Channel. Sadly, her mother died when Lynch was a baby, and she was raised by an aunt and uncle, spending much of her childhood traveling around Asia. When she was eight, she saw yoga for the first time and was fascinated. At the time, yoga was practiced mostly by men, but that didn't stop her. She liked to break down barriers and worked for human rights with Gandhi, MLK, and Charles de Gaulle. She relocated to the U.S. and immediately went to Hollywood, continuing with her yoga and often teaching her costars. In her late forties, she gave up acting to focus on yoga full time. She co-founded the Yoga Teachers Alliance (now the Yoga Teachers Association) and is the Guinness World Record holder for oldest yoga teacher. At age eighty-seven, Lynch decided it was time for something new. She began competitive ballroom dancing and was an absolute natural, taking home piles of trophies and often partnering with dancers seventy years her junior.

88

88

THE YEAR OF THE SPIDERS, BUT LIKE, GOOD SPIDERS

Have you ever thought, "Hmmm, what am I really afraid of? What do I really love? How can I combine these two things into something terrifying and unmissable? Would it perhaps best be expressed as a horrifying thirty-foot spider that represents my loving and complicated relationship with my mother?" If the answer is yes, then wow. Do you need a hug?

This is your year to embrace your inner fears and turn them inside out. Set yourself free. And remember: If spiders can poop silk, then you can build anything.

* * *

Louise Bourgeois got her artistic start restoring tapestries for her parents' business. Louise's mother died shortly before Louise went to study math at the Sorbonne, and Louise ultimately abandoned her pursuit of math to focus on her first love, art. She moved to New York City and continued to explore themes of femininity, domesticity, sexuality, and the body in her art. At age thirty-four, Bourgeois had her first solo exhibit, mostly of prints, but the art world took little notice. When she was in her early forties, she transitioned to working more exclusively in sculpture. When she was sixty-seven, she received her first public sculpture commission. By age seventy, her notoriety had continued to grow and she won a retrospective at The Museum of Modern Art in New York. At age eighty-eight, she created her seminal work, *Maman*, a thirty-foot spider cast in bronze, steel, and marble. An ode to her mother, *Maman* has been exhibited all over the world, creeping out audiences around the globe. Thank you for your brilliant brain, Bourgeois.

89

89

THE BEAUTIFUL STRAIGHT LINE YEAR

You might think this cosmic journey called existence is a winding road, but it's actually a beautiful straight line. The universe is full of gorgeous math and geometry and also people who are absolute butts and don't want you to succeed.

But you know what's important to you, what you want to create. It may take some time, but if you truly believe it, keep following that line and be patient as your people find you.

* * *

Carmen Herrera was born in Cuba but spent her formative years moving between Cuba and France, taking art lessons wherever she went. At the age of thirty-three, she became fascinated by the world of geometry, angles, and straight lines while studying architecture. She moved to Paris and continued her art studies with a focus on painting and printmaking, and she was part of an exhibit at the Salon des Réalités Nouvelles, though she did not gain broad recognition. Herrera moved to New York and soon found her minimalist art style was ahead of its time. She faced significant discrimination in the art world as a woman and an immigrant, and the critics were unkind. Herrera did not let this deter her and she continued to paint, mastering crisp lines and contrasting vibrant planes. At age eighty-nine, she sold her first painting, then went on to have several museum and gallery exhibits, including a solo retrospective at the Whitney Museum of American Art when she was 101.

90

THE TRUEST SELF YEAR

You know who you are. You've always known. It's about time the world knows too.

Society makes all kinds of decisions for us: how to behave, who to be, what time of year you're able to buy Girl Scout Cookies. (Free the cookies! Thin Mints are not seasonal!) This is your year to take a step back and ask, am I doing this because it's who I am, or am I doing this because it's what I *think* the world wants me to do?

Screw the world! Don't waste time being anything other than yourself. Find your name and shout it loud!

Also, Thin Mints freeze really well, so stock up.

* * *

Patricia Davis realized at the age of three that her gender and sex didn't match. She didn't have the words to describe what she was feeling, not even hearing the word "transgender" until she was well into her forties. It took another twenty years for her to say it out loud. When she was sixty, she came out to her wife, who was supportive and quietly bought Davis dresses and jewelry, but ultimately, they decided to keep Patricia a secret from their friends and neighbors. When Davis's wife died, she decided it was time to come out. At age ninety, she was finally able to be her truest self.

91

91

THE BALANCING ACT YEAR

Life is all about finding balance. Sometimes you find it leaping through the air, sometimes you find it somersaulting on a ridiculously narrow beam, and sometimes you find it by reclaiming something you once loved.

This is your year to step into the limelight, roll with your dreams, and discover what it means to truly have balance. And if you happen to *crush* the competition, and expectations, while walking on your hands . . . even better!

* * *

Johanna Quaas was an active child and started learning gymnastics at a young age in Germany in the 1930s, but she had to quit when *something* (asshole Nazis) prevented her from continuing to train. She missed her chance, but as an adult she channeled her love of the sport into teaching and coaching, leading several other gymnasts and teams to victory. But when Quaas turned fifty-six, she realized there was nothing stopping her from being the one doing all the fun flippy things. She started training again and went on to win the German Senior Gymnastics Championship in her age group eleven times in a row. At the age of ninety-one, she competed in her last competition, going out on top.

92

92

THE OVER THE PLATE YEAR

Heeey batter batter, saw-wiiing batter bat . . . oh, you have to leave? Now? But you just wound up the pitch. No, it's okay, I get it. Saving the world is important too. I'll just stand here 'til you're ready. Oh, you won't be back for seventy-three years? No, it's okay. I'll wait. I've got a book.

Just when you think you've got everything all figured out, the world feels like it's at war. Or maybe the world *is* at war and you get called to fight. Don't feel like you struck out just because you decided to sit out a few games. Don't give up on your dream. Pick that ball back up and throw it right over the plate.

* * *

Anthony I. "Tony" Gianunzio's dreams came true at the age of nineteen when he was scouted by the Chicago Cubs to be a pitcher. But it was 1942 and WWII reared its head. Instead of playing for the Cubs, Gianunzio joined the military, serving in the U.S. Coast Guard in the terrifying Pacific Theater. He survived but assumed his dream had drifted away for good. When the war finally ended, he turned his focus toward teaching high school. For the next four-plus decades, he taught English in Michigan. After he retired, someone at the Chicago Cubs heard Gianunzio's story of sacrifice and invited him to fulfill his dream. At age ninety-two, he threw out the first pitch at Wrigley Field.

93

93

THE MAJOR MAYOR YEAR

Kiss dem babies! Shake dem hands! Campaign for yourself. Don't be afraid to take charge of your life or perhaps your co-op board or even your town or state.

The best way to make your world better is to get involved. Don't hesitate to make it yours.

* * *

Dorothy Geeben moved in the 1950s to the retirement community of Ocean Breeze, Florida—population 463. Her husband passed away soon after they relocated, leaving Geeben with lots of time on her hands. She believed the secret to a long life was keeping busy, and she became a fixture in the local community—teaching craft classes, gambling . . . uh, going to bingo games, and playing the organ at her church. Geeben realized she could make a difference by participating in the local government. She began her political career by winning a spot on the city council—a position she held for over thirty years—before being voted in as the country's oldest active mayor at the age of ninety-three. Geeben even won all her re-election campaigns and remained mayor until she was 101.

94

THE METAL YEAR

GAAAAAARRRRR!!!! SCREW NAZIS! SAVE POLAR BEARS! BE KIND TO YOUR BRAIN! DON'T FEAR DEATH! DEATH FEARS YOU! DON'T BE AFRAID TO RAISE YOUR VOICE! A LOT! THE MOST METAL THING YOU CAN DO IS BE YOURSELF! THAT OR SNORTING A ROW OF ANTS! BUT BEING YOURSELF IS MUCH MORE FUN!

* * *

Inge Ginsberg was born into an affluent Jewish family in Vienna in 1922 but had to flee her homeland because of those damn Nazis (who ruined so many childhoods in this book!). But Ginsberg wasn't going to go quietly, and she spent the rest of WWII working with the Italian resistance smuggling weapons, intelligence, and even people. After the war, she and her husband moved to Hollywood with the dream of becoming singer/songwriters. Ginsberg found Hollywood fake, divorced her husband, and moved to Zurich. She found work as a writer and real estate investor and was a wiz at the stock market. She made a great life for herself that consisted of traveling and falling in love. After her third husband died, she started to split her time between New York City, Israel, and Switzerland. It was in New York that she met and befriended her future bandmates, musicians Lucia Caruso and Pedro da Silva. Ginsberg had always loved poetry and shared a piece she had written with her friends about death. Da Silva realized it would make a killer song, and their band, Inge and the Tritone Kings, was formed with Ginsberg at the screaming center. They competed on *Switzerland's Got Talent* and entered the Eurovision song contest, catching the world's attention, not just for the novelty of a ninety-four-year-old frontwoman for a metal band but also for the deep themes of Ginsberg's songs: death, escaping the Nazis, the Holocaust, climate change, and mental health. Turns out there's a whole lot to scream about.

95

95

THE COMMENCEMENT YEAR

Good morning, students. I know you have a massive headache from last night's game of beer pong, but pick your head up off that coconut water and realize how lucky you are to learn. You get to hear thrilling stories from history that connect human experiences. You get to look at great works of art and decide how they make you feel inside. You get to calculus with calculus so you can, uh . . . numbers better, which will help you on a daily basis we're sure.

Life only gets boring when you stop learning. The easiest way to feel young is to keep your brain fresh. Consider taking a class at a local university or listening to some lectures; watch some documentaries and read some nonfiction. Get in touch with your inner student . . . but maybe avoid the keg stand part.

* * *

Nola Ochs was born in Kansas before the Great Depression. She followed the expected path: get married, have kids, work on your family farm. But Ochs desperately loved to learn. She took college courses via correspondence and got a teaching certificate, but life got in the way and she didn't finish her actual degree. When she was in her early sixties, her husband died, and she found herself with spare time. She began taking classes at the local community college, signing up for whatever courses sounded interesting to her without thinking about a degree. A professor noticed and discovered that she was just one credit short of an associate's degree. She took that one missing piece—an algebra class—and graduated at the age of seventy-seven. But she didn't feel done, so Ochs re-enrolled at Fort Hayes State University, the same college where she'd taken classes nearly sixty years earlier. She started with online classes but decided she wanted the full college experience and moved 100 miles from the family farm and into campus housing. She graduated at age ninety-five, with a 3.7 GPA and the love and adoration of her fellow students.

96

96

THE CRACK IN THE WALL YEAR

The world is full of walls. Many of them are quite visible and relatively uncomfortable to walk into. But it's the metaphorical ones that are more painful to smash your face against. Walls can *grow*, and they will grow around you if you sit too long doubting yourself. Don't fear them. You might have to collide with the same wall over and over again, but at some point, a small delicate crack will appear.

Now hit it with a hammer! Kick it! Smash it! Run through it like the Kool-Aid Man, leaving a hole in the shape of your triumphant body! Then use the experience as fodder for a super lovely novel.

* * *

Harry Bernstein grew up exceptionally poor, the child of Jewish immigrants from Poland who found themselves in a northern English mill town. His street was divided between Christians and Jews with unspoken rules about crossing between the two. Bernstein had a love of writing, moved to Chicago, and penned his first novel . . . only to have it rejected. He needed to support his family, so he worked as a freelancer, selling stories to various magazines and newspapers, until he eventually landed a steady job as an editor at a trade magazine. When Bernstein was in his early seventies, he got his first publishing deal with the novel *The Smile*. Sadly, it was nothing to smile about because it sold very poorly. His wife passed away when he was in his early nineties. Overwhelmed with grief, he spiraled into thoughts of the past and began to write about the street he grew up on, creating what would become *The Invisible Wall*. The book talked of his abusive father, the religious discord, the plights of workers, and at the core, a *Romeo and Juliet*–style love story inspired by his own sister's real-life secret relationship with a Christian boy across the street. He submitted his book to several New York publishers who turned it down, and it sat in unsolicited piles for years before finally being published by Random House to great acclaim when Bernstein was ninety-six.

97

97

THE BOOGIE ON YEAR

The beat starts the moment you're born. Most people ignore it, the ba-dum-ba-dum that pulses through our veins. It's the rare soul who leans into the rhythm and learns to make it their own.

Life may try to distract you from the music—the loud sound of being ignored, the roar of being overlooked, the scream of an occasional knife fight—but step back and really listen. Ba-dum-ba-dum. It's always inside you. Don't be afraid to boogie on.

* * *

Joe Willie "Pinetop" Perkins was born in 1913 in Mississippi and raised on a plantation. He began his musical career playing guitar, but the tendons in his left arm were injured during a knife fight with a dancer at a juke joint and he switched to playing the piano. He found work in radio shows and eventually got a touring gig with Earl Hooker. Perkins's first popular single was a cover of Clarence "Pinetop" Smith's song, "The Pinetop Boogie-Woogie," earning him his lifelong moniker, Pinetop. After his common-law wife died, he slipped into alcoholic depression and considered quitting music. But the legendary Muddy Waters was a fan, and after he lost his piano player, he asked Perkins to join his blues band. For the next four decades, Pinetop worked as a "sideman" (aka studio musician) on countless albums but did not record an album of his own. When he finally got the courage, he couldn't stop and recorded nearly twenty albums, capping his career at age ninety-seven by winning a Grammy for Best Traditional Blues Album for *Joined at the Hip* with Willie "Big Eyes" Smith. The feat made him the oldest Grammy Award winner ever.

98

98

THE EYE TO THE FUTURE YEAR

You've spent your entire life honing your craft. So what if people haven't caught on to your absolute brilliance yet? So what if the critics don't understand your vision? So what if your friend with a strangely sexy unibrow gets way more famous than you?

Don't stop. Keep your eye to the future because you never know what's around the corner.

* * *

Luchita Hurtado was born in 1920 in Venezuela and later settled in New York City. She got married and had kids, but her husband abandoned them, and she turned to her creative abilities to support her family. She found work painting department store murals and earned money doing fashion illustration as well. Hurtado bounced around with jobs between Mexico, California, and New Mexico, all the while creating art in multiple mediums that often referenced her own body, the environment, and feminism. During this time, she befriended the legendary Frida Kahlo, and while Hurtado's work was sporadically exhibited, she didn't receive the kind of recognition her friend did. It wasn't until she was in her late nineties that art critics discovered her earlier work and the fact that she was still creating. At age ninety-eight, she was finally granted her first large solo exhibition—*I Live, I Die, I Will Be Reborn*—which opened at The Serpentine Gallery in London.

99

THE NOT QUITE PEAK YEAR

There's that song that tells you to climb every mountain. Well, screw that! Some mountains aren't worth your time. Some mountains are only like one thousand feet. Pah! You can handle mountains twelve times as high!

Choose your mountain. Maybe it's the tallest, maybe it's the steepest, maybe it's the one with the cutest animals (pikas!). Maybe it's the mountain that's been in your backyard this whole time, staring at you, waiting for you to connect with it and touch the sky. Slap on your favorite hiking socks and climb higher than you ever thought you could.

* * *

Teiichi Igarashi, an eighty-nine-year-old retired lumberjack and forest ranger, decided to climb Mount Fuji in memory of his recently deceased wife. At 12,388 feet, the climb was no easy stroll, but Igarashi made it to the summit and then made it a yearly pilgrimage, trekking his way up the mountain wearing only thick socks—no shoes—and carrying a picture of his beloved. His family—his children *and* grandchildren—started to join in his climbs. He continued this yearly trek for over a decade and broke the record for the oldest person to climb Mount Fuji—and should have also won an award for some impressively tough feet.

100

100
THE TRY AND KEEP UP YEAR

TRIPLE DIGITS, BABY!!! You've reached an elite club. Your velvet jacket is in the mail. (That's a thing, right?)

People will underestimate you. But you've mastered the art of life. You know more than any double-digit plebian, and don't you forget it. Wake up every morning and smile because it's a day of possibility. You've got all the achievement points, but it's never too late to keep leveling up. Life is a marathon, and you're killing this race.

* * *

Fauja Singh was born with weak legs and couldn't walk until he was five years old. As a child, he was often bullied because of his legs. He tried to take up running in his twenties as a way to strengthen them but ultimately gave it up. In his eighties, Singh tragically witnessed the death of one of his sons, and he turned to running to help deal with his grief. After a few years, he began running seriously—training for and running in his first race, the London friggin' Marathon. At age one hundred, Singh attempted and achieved eight world records in one day: the 100-meter, 200-meter, 400-meter, 800-meter, 1500-meter, 1-mile, 3,000-meter, and 5,000-meter records in his age bracket. Three days later, he became the first one-hundred-year-old to complete a full marathon. At the time of this writing, he is 111 years old and going strong.

100+

100+
YOUR YEAR

The story doesn't stop here! The one thing this world is never without is possibility. Write your own entry and remember it's never too late to follow your dreams.

Unless your dreams are about spiders, dolls, or other terrifying things (see entries 88 and 49). We'd prefer fewer of those.

ABOUT THE AUTHORS

Colleen AF Venable

At age thirty-nine, four years after Colleen was all whiny about being too old, she published *Kiss Number 8*, which was nominated for the National Book Award and an Eisner, won the Mosaic Award, and was a Prism Award finalist and a *Publishers Weekly* Best Book. A two-decade veteran of publishing, she's designed hundreds of award-winning graphic novels for First Second Books, was Creative Director at Workman Publishing, started Macmillan's Odd Dot imprint, and now works as Director of Epic Originals. Her other talents include accidentally inventing national holidays (National Pancake Day, September 26th) with great friends like Meghan.

Meghan Daly

At age thirty-five, Meghan's "Swayze Year," she changed careers from working in corporate America to opening up a beloved pie shop in Brooklyn, NY. Daly Pie has been featured in the *New York Times*, Eater, and on The Cooking Channel (twice). At age thirty-nine, Meghan embraced change once again and wrote her first book with her best friend, Colleen.